W9-BFR-775

Thank you for worshipping with us!

www.kingswaychurch.org
317.272.2222

Glimpses

Concept, design and production by Left Coast Design, Portland, Oregon.

Photography by Greg Whitaker, Columbus, Indiana.

ISBN: 0-89221-487-2

Library of Congress: 99-69238

Printed in the United States of America.

Please visit our website for other great titles: *www.newleafpress.net*

For information regarding publicity contact

Dianna Fletcher at 870-438-5288

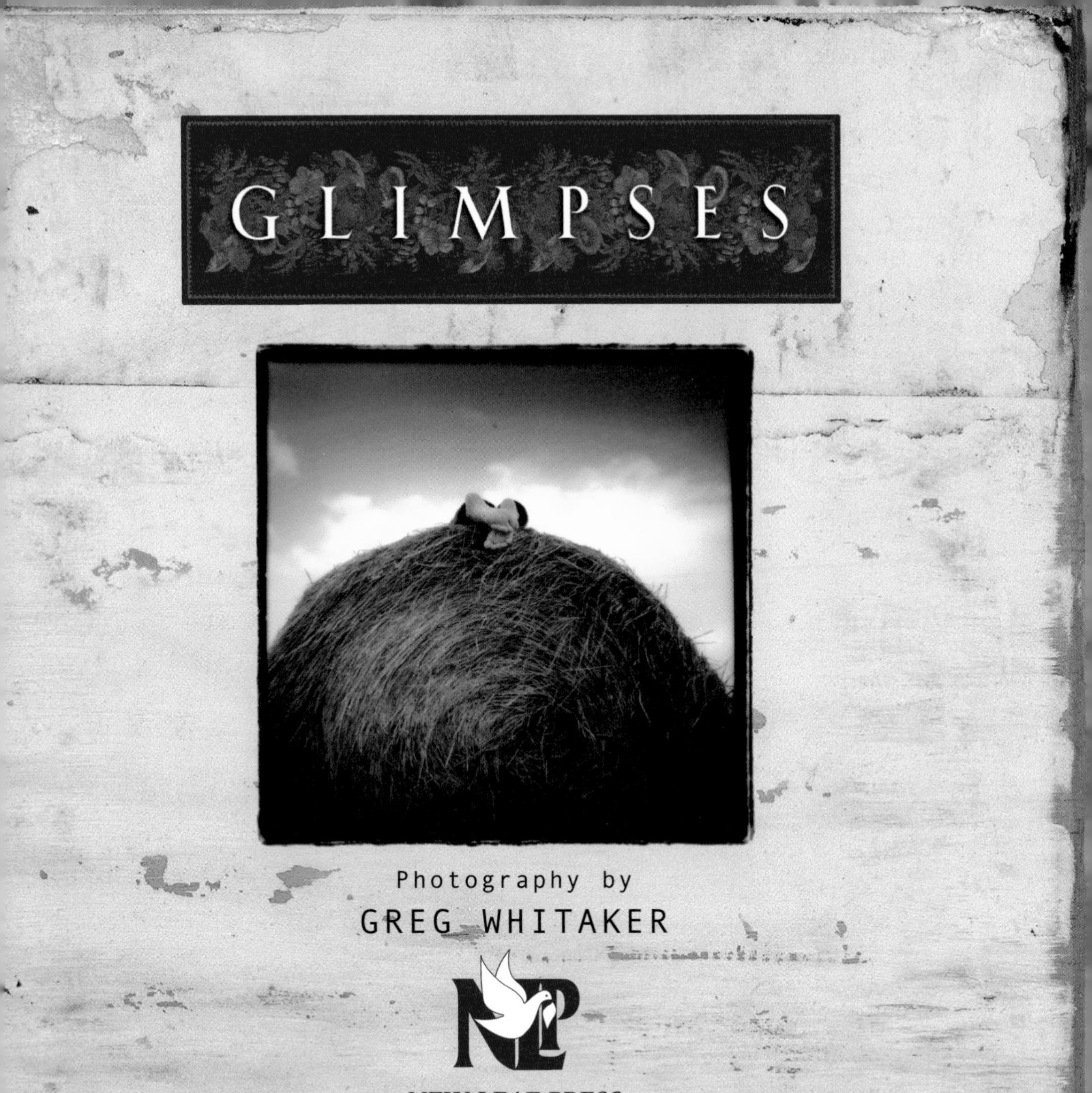

www.newleafpress.net

PROVERBS 12:25

Anxiety in the heart of a man weighs it down. But a good word makes it glad.

PROVERBS 4:20-22

My son, pay attention to what I say; listen closely to my words. Do not let them out of your sight; Keep them within your heart. For they are life to those who find them, and health to a man's whole body.

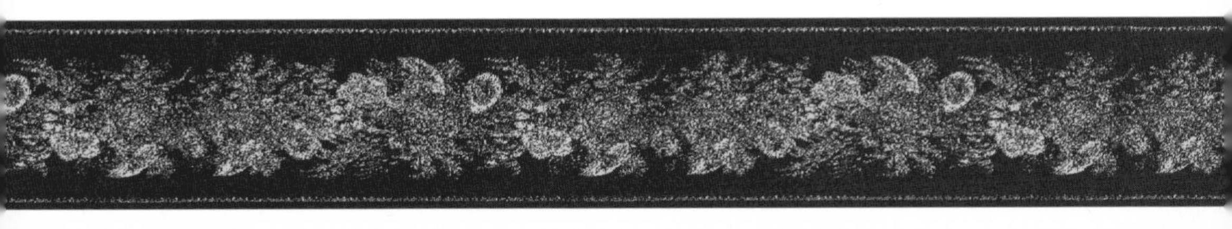

PSALM 39:1

I will guard my ways, that I may not sin with my tongue, I will guard my mouth as with a muzzle.

Wounds from a friend are better
than kisses from an enemy!

LUKE 18:16

Let the little children come to me! Never send them away! For the Kingdom of God belongs to men who have hearts as trusting as these little children's. Anyone who doesn't have their kind of faith will never get within the kingdom's gates.

PSALM 59:1

Deliver me from my enemies, O my God; set me securely on high away from those who rise up against me.

PSALM 34:4

I sought the Lord, and He answered me,

and delivered me from all my fears.

PROVERBS 13:22

A good man leaves an inheritance

to his children's children..

I waited patiently for God to help me;

He listened and heard my cry.

Listen, my son, accept what I say, and the years of your life will be many.

I guide you in the way of wisdom

and lead you along straight paths.

When you walk, your
steps will not be
hampered;

when you run,
you will not
stumble.

PSALM 92:1

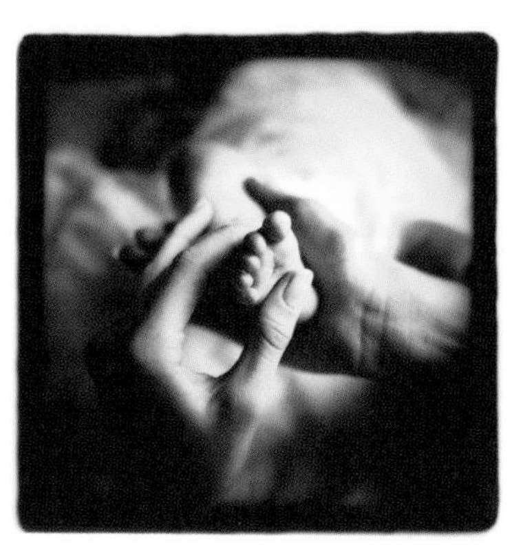

It is good to say "thank you" to the Lord.

PROVERBS 14:29, 30

A wise man controls his temper. He knows that anger causes mistakes. A relaxed attitude lengthens a man's life; jealousy rots it away

A tranquil heart is life to the body.

JOSHUA 14:10-11

Now then, just as the Lord promised, he has kept me alive for forty-five years since the time he said this to Moses, while Israel moved about in the desert. So here I am today, eighty-five years old! I am still as strong today as the day Moses sent me out; I'm just as vigorous to go out to battle now as I was then.

The man who knows right from wrong and has good judgement and common sense is happier than the man who is immensely rich! For such wisdom is far more valuable than precious jewels. Nothing else compares with it.

There is one who pretends to be rich, but has nothing; Another pretends to be poor, but has great wealth.

ECCLESIASTES 3:1,2

There is an appointed time for everything.

A time to sow and a time to reap.

PROVERBS 12:4

An excellent wife is the

crown of her husband…

PROVERBS 18:22

He who finds a wife finds a good thing,

and obtains favor from the Lord.

PSALM 37:4

Delight yourself in the Lord;

and He will give you the

desires of you heart.

PROVERBS 23:15-16

My son, how I will rejoice if you become a man of common sense. Yes, my heart will thrill to your thoughtful, wise words.

PROVERBS 13:18

Poverty and shame will come to Him who neglects discipline.

But he who regards reproof will be honored.

PROVERBS 23:24, 25

The father of the righteous

will greatly rejoice…

Let your father and mother be glad

Praise the Lord from the heavens,

Praise Him in the heights!

Praise Him, all his angels,

Praise Him, all His hosts!

Praise Him, sun and moon;

Praise Him, all stars

of light!

He will bless those who fear the Lord, small and great alike.

By wisdom a house is built, and
by understanding it is established; and
by knowledge the rooms are filled with
all precious and pleasant riches.

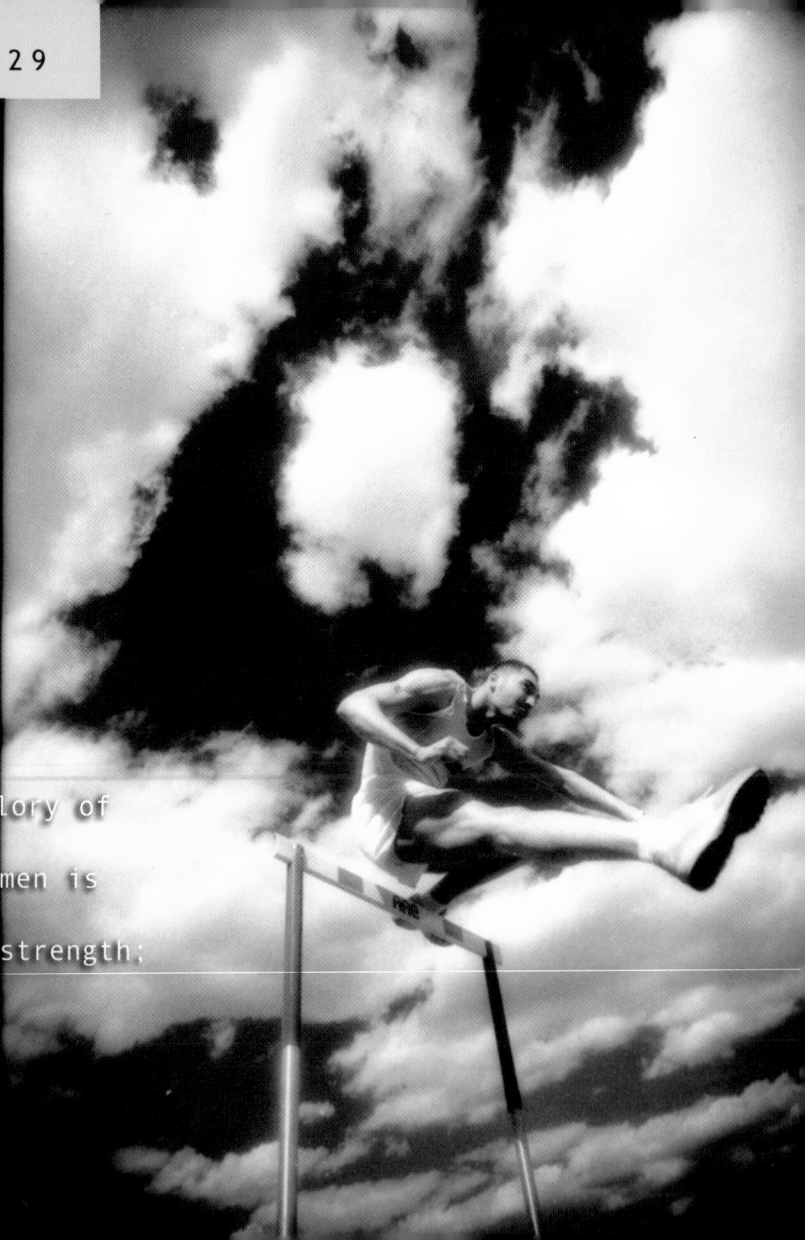

The glory of
young men is
their strength;

of old men, their experience.

A happy heart makes the face cheerful, but heartache crushes the spirit.

PROVERBS 4:23

Watch over your heart with
all diligence, for from it flow
the springs of life.

PSALM 28:5

They care nothing for God or what He has done or what He has made;

Therefore God will dismantle them like old,

buildings, never to be rebuilt again.

PROVERBS 14:23

Work brings profit; talk brings poverty!

PSALM 131:2

I have stilled and quieted my soul; like a weaned child with its mother. . . is my soul within me.

A man's pride will bring him low, but

a humble spirit will obtain honor.

Plans fail for lack of counsel,

but with many advisers they succeed.

PROVERBS 3:5,6

Trust in the Lord with all your heart, do not

ean on your own understanding.

In all your ways acknowledge Him, and He will make your paths straight.

PROVERBS 22:6

Train up a child in the way he should go, even when he is old he will not depart from it.

How can a young man keep his way pure?

By keeping it according to thy word.

Is not wisdom found among the aged?

Does not long life bring understanding?

PSALMS 51:6-7

You deserve honesty
from the heart: yes, utter
sincerity and truthfulness.
Oh, give me this wisdom.
Sprinkle me with the
cleansing blood and I shall
be clean again. Wash me
and I shall be whiter
than snow.

PSALM 32:8

I will instruct you and teach you in the way which you should go; I will counsel you and watch over you.

PSALM 4:8

I will lie down and sleep in peace, for you alone, O Lord, make me dwell in safety.

JEREMIAH 33:3

Call to Me, and I will answer you, and I will tell you great and mighty things, which you do not know.

PSALM 127:3

Children are

a gift from

God; they are

His reward.

PROVERBS 3:11,12

My son, do not despise the Lord's
discipline and do not resent His rebuke,
because the Lord disciplines those He loves,
as a father the son he delights in.

There is a way which seems right to a man, but its end is the way of death.

GREG WHITAKER

With a black and white photograph, I feel that I have the ability to deepen the level of interpretation of the original scene that I saw through the lens, the ability to distill the image down to what is really important. Hopefully, if I have done it well, I can help the viewer feel some of what I felt when I looked upon the scene or into the eyes of the subject. My aim is to make a picture that is honest and evokes emotion, not through manipulation or deception, but by conveying some of the dignity, which I feel, exist in simple life and everyday people.

Greg Whitaker is a freelance photographer who resides in a “project-oriented” 125 year old farmhouse in rural Indiana with his wife. His commercial work takes him around the United States for various agencies while his first love remains black and white portraiture. It was that body of work that captured the attention of Left Coast Design, a graphic design company with deep roots in book publishing located in Portland, Oregon. Left Coast created the *Glimpses* concept combining Whitaker’s poignant photos with the simple truths of the Bible.